He was not very tall, but very stocky and strong, with a cruel and terrible appearance, a long straight nose, distended nostrils, a thin and reddish face in which the large, wide-open green eyes were framed by bushy black eyebrows, which made them appear threatening. . . . A bull's neck supported the head, from which black curly locks were falling to his wide-shouldered person.

Nicholas of Modrussa,
a representative of the Pope, 1464,
describing Vlad the Impaler

This book is for Allan and Leonore.

Photographs © 2008: akg-Images, London: 70 bottom, 113 (Paul Almasy), 55, 66 top; Alamy Images: 69 center (Mihai Florin), 73 top left, 73 right (KPA Honorar & Belege/Content Mine International), 72 top right (Mary Evans Picture Library), 118 (Massimo Pizzocaro), 103 (Kristen Soper), 14, 69 top, 71 bottom, 80, 117 (The Marsden Archive), 10 (The Print Collector), 96 (Visual Arts Library, London), 110 (Richard Wareham Fotografie), 40, 70 center (Tim E. White); Bridgeman Art Library International Ltd., London/New York: 72 bottom (Bibliotheque Nationale, Paris, France/Archives Charmet), 19 (Bibliotheque Polonaise, Paris, France/ Archives Charmet), 34, 67 top (Stapleton Collection, UK), 50, 69 bottom, 77, 83 (The Marsden Archive, UK); Corbis Images: 29, 59, 62, 65, 68 top, 72 top left, 73 bottom left (Bettmann), 53 (Philip de Bay/Historical Picture Archive), 61 (Otto Lang), 57 (Underwood & Underwood), 66 bottom (Sandro Vannini); Getty Images/David Greedy: 71 top; Mary Evans Picture Library: 45, 68 bottom, 101; Superstock, Inc./age fotostock: 26; The Granger Collection, New York: 70 top, 91; The Image Works/Fotomas/Topham: 33, 67 bottom.

Illustrations by XNR Productions, Inc.: 4, 5, 8, 9
Cover art by Mark Summers
Chapter art for chapters 4, 7, 11, 12, 13 by Roland Sarkany
Chapter art for chapters 1, 2, 3, 5, 6, 8, 9, 10, 14, 15 by Raphael Montoliu

Library of Congress Cataloging-in-Publication Data

Goldberg, Enid A.
Vlad the impaler : the real Count Dracula / Enid A. Goldberg & Norman Itzkowitz.
p. cm. — (A wicked history)
Includes bibliographical references and index.
ISBN-13: 978-0-531-12599-1 (lib. bdg.) 978-0-531-13898-4 (pbk.)
ISBN-10: 0-531-12599-8 (lib. bdg.) 0-531-13898-4 (pbk.)
1. Vlad III, Prince of Wallachia, 1430 or 31-1476 or 7—Juvenile
literature. 2. Wallachia—Kings and rulers—Biography—Juvenile
literature. 3. Wallachia—History—Juvenile literature. 4. Dracula,
Count (Fictitious character)—Juvenile literature. I. Itzkowitz,
Norman. II. Title.
DR240.5.V55G65 2007
949.8'2014092—dc22
[B]

2007016144

Tod Olson, Series Editor
Marie O'Neill, Art Director
Allicette Torres, Cover Design
SimonSays Design!, Book Design and Production

© 2008 Scholastic Inc.

1 2 3 4 5 6 7 8 9 10 R 17 16 15 14 13 12 11 10 09 08   23

Vlad the Impaler

The Real Count Dracula

ENID A. GOLDBERG &
NORMAN ITZKOWITZ

Franklin Watts
An Imprint of Scholastic Inc.
New York   Toronto   London   Auckland   Sydney
Mexico City   New Delhi   Hong Kong
Danbury, Connecticut

The World of Vlad Dracula

During his brutal career, Vlad usually backed the Holy Roman Empire against the Ottoman Turks. But he lashed out against his allies, too.

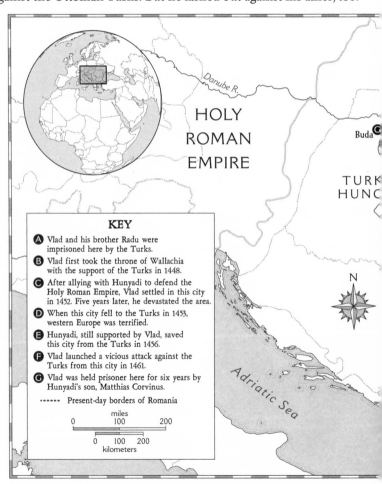

HOLY ROMAN EMPIRE

Danube R.

Buda **C**

TURK
HUN C

KEY

A Vlad and his brother Radu were imprisoned here by the Turks.

B Vlad first took the throne of Wallachia with the support of the Turks in 1448.

C After allying with Hunyadi to defend the Holy Roman Empire, Vlad settled in this city in 1452. Five years later, he devastated the area.

D When this city fell to the Turks in 1453, western Europe was terrified.

E Hunyadi, still supported by Vlad, saved this city from the Turks in 1456.

F Vlad launched a vicious attack against the Turks from this city in 1461.

G Vlad was held prisoner here for six years by Hunyadi's son, Matthias Corvinus.

‑‑‑‑‑‑ Present-day borders of Romania

```
            miles
0         100        200

    0    100   200
       kilometers
```

N

Adriatic Sea

TABLE OF CONTENTS

PART 4: THE FINAL YEARS

A Wicked Web

A look at the allies and enemies of Vlad the Impaler.

Vlad's Family

⌣⌣⌣⌣⌣⌣⌣⌣⌣⌣⌣⌣⌣

VLAD DRACUL
Vlad the Impaler's father; ruled
Wallachia from 1436–1447

RADU
one of Vlad's younger
brothers; would lead a
rebellion against him

BOGDAN II
a relative by marriage; ruler of
Moldavia

MIRCEA
one of Vlad's older brothers;
brutally tortured and buried
alive

VLAD THE MONK
Vlad's half brother

STEPHEN OF MOLDAVIA
son of Bogdan II; Vlad's cousin

Leaders Within Wallachia

⌣⌣⌣⌣⌣⌣⌣⌣⌣⌣⌣⌣⌣

THE BOYARS
nobles; lifelong enemies
of Vlad

DAN III
Vladislav II's brother

VLADISLAV II
dethroned by Vlad in
1456

BASARAB LAIOTA
successor and possible
murderer of Vlad

VLAD THE IMPAI
also known as Vlad Drac
Prince of Wallachia three

Leaders from the Ottoman Empire

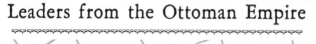

SULTAN MURAD II
head of the Ottoman Empire;
imprisoned Vlad and his
brother Radu

SULTAN MOHAMMED II
Murad's son; leader of the
Ottomans after Murad's death

Leaders from the Holy Roman Empire

JÁNOS HUNYADI
selected to lead the fight against
the Ottoman Turks; sometime ally,
sometime enemy of Vlad

MATTHIAS CORVINUS
Hunyadi's son; also an ally
and enemy of Vlad

VLAD DRACULA (1431–1476)

THE CARPATHIAN MOUNTAINS stretch across the Romanian region of Transylvania. They are deeply wooded, green and beautiful by day. At night the hills turn dark and lonely. Wolves howl. Bats soar. Spooky mists rise out of mountain lakes.

It's a perfect setting for one of the most famous horror stories of all time: Bram Stoker's *Dracula*. In the novel, a dark castle stands on a narrow pass in the Carpathians. Inside its cold stone walls lives a tall old man dressed in black from head to toe. He is a Transylvanian count with a polite manner—and a taste for human blood. By day he sleeps in his coffin. At night he rises to look for victims. He attacks with a bite to the neck. Each victim becomes, like the count himself, a vampire.

Count Dracula is a product of Stoker's imagination. But deep in those same mountains there once lived a real

Dracula. In the 1400s, he was prince of Wallachia, the land next to Transylvania. And he ruled with a thirst for blood worthy of a vampire. The story of his life may have inspired Stoker when he sat down to write his book.

But the story of Vlad Dracula, Prince of Wallachia, is more gruesome than any horror tale. In a few short years in power, he claimed more victims than Stoker's vampire. And he used a method far bloodier than a bite to the neck—a method that earned him the nickname Vlad the Impaler.

In a life devoted to cruelty, one event stands out above the others. The year was probably 1457. Vlad had been prince of Wallachia for just seven months. On Easter Sunday, he decided to announce his arrival.

According to one account, Vlad invited 200 boyars, or local leaders, to a feast. They gathered at his castle in Targoviste. Many of Wallachia's wealthy landowners were there. In a large dining hall, Vlad served them plenty of food. There was dancing and music.

But despite the royal welcome, there must have been tension in the air. Traditionally, the boyars had been enemies of Vlad's family. Ten years earlier, when Vlad's father ruled Wallachia, the boyars had revolted against the family. They chased Vlad's father and brother out of the capital. The rebels buried Vlad's brother alive in the hills. Not long after, they shot his father.

If the boyars thought that Vlad had forgotten these murders, they were wrong. As the boyars began to leave the feast, Vlad's guards surrounded them. In an instant, the guests became prisoners.

The prince questioned his captives. He singled out the boyars who were old enough to have been involved in the revolt. Then he had the guards carry out his orders.

The prisoners were led outside the city walls. If they really numbered in the hundreds, the executions must have taken a long time. The last victims had to watch in terror for hours. One by one, the prisoners were impaled—run through with sharp stakes.

As the killings went on, the soil around Targoviste grew muddy with blood. Terrible cries of pain drifted over the city walls. Most of the prisoners did not die right away.

AFTER THE BRUTAL SLAYING OF THE BOYARS, the grounds of Vlad's castle (background) were said to be muddy with blood.

When the killing finally ended, Dracula had the stakes propped up outside the city. He arranged them in orderly patterns. There, above the hills, the bodies of Targoviste's leading citizens slowly rotted. Blackbirds flocked around the corpses, fighting for a meal.

This was the scene that greeted visitors to Wallachia's capital. Travelers approached the city's gates through a maze of horrors that became known as the Forest of the Impaled. It's possible to imagine what went through their minds: What offense could bring this kind of treatment on a person? Why would someone choose this kind of punishment, then display his victims for all to see? Who is the evil prince that rules this city? Centuries from now, will the world still remember his cruelty?

PART 1

The Making

of a

Monster

Little Devil

Vlad Dracul has a son and takes a
vow to DEFEND AN EMPIRE.

THE YEAR WAS 1431. There was reason for excitement
in a three-story stucco house in Sighisoara, Transylvania.
A baby boy had just been born. His mother's name has
been lost to history. His father came from a family of
princes in the neighboring state of Wallachia. He passed
his own name, Vlad, on to his second son.

The elder Vlad must have been proud, of his son
and himself. In February of the same year, he had
traveled 700 miles to receive a great honor. He and 23
other men gathered in the city of Nuremberg. They

came from Europe's most important royal families. Each had been specially chosen by Emperor Sigismund. As head of the Holy Roman Empire, Sigismund held power over much of western Europe. These 24 men were to be his trusted knights.

Vlad and the others entered a chapel in the imperial fortress. They knelt at the emperor's feet. In a quiet ceremony, they swore loyalty to Sigismund. And they became members of the Order of the Dragon.

VLAD'S FATHER, VLAD DRACUL, became one of Emperor Sigismund's knights. He promised to protect the Holy Roman Empire. It was a vow that Vlad Dracul would break again and again.

Like the others, Vlad received a green cape and a black cape. He was given a medallion with an image of a dragon engraved on it. He also received a promise he had desperately wanted. The emperor vowed to make him prince of Wallachia.

In return, Vlad and the other knights made an important pledge. They swore to defend the empire and the Christian faith from its enemies. It was a vital task because a crisis was closing in on Western Europe from the east.

For 200 years, Turkish tribes had been gathering power in western Asia. Little by little, the Turks were taking over the Byzantine Empire. The empire was a 1,000-year-old Christian power that lay to the southeast of Sigismund's empire.

By 1431, most Byzantine cities were controlled by the Turkish sultan, Murad II. The sultan ruled over a new power in the region: the Ottoman Empire. Its official faith was not Christianity, but Islam.

From his palace in Nuremberg, Sigismund understood the problem. The Ottoman Turks were closing in on the Byzantine capital of Constantinople. No one knew how long the city would hold out. If it fell, many people worried that the Turks would sweep into western Europe.

With them would come the signs of their religious faith. They would build mosques near ancient Christian churches. They would hold prayer sessions in public. The Turks were generally more tolerant of other faiths than Christian rulers were. But in the view of Emperor Sigismund, Christianity was in terrible danger.

Vlad lived near the first line of defense. Sighisoara rested on a northern slope of the Carpathian Mountains. On the other side of the mountains lay Wallachia. To the south of Wallachia were the Turks.

Vlad returned from Nuremberg to take up his new duties as defender of the Empire. Sighisoara was perfect for the purpose. A seven-foot-thick stone wall surrounded the city. Guards stored weapons in rooms carved into the wall. Soldiers kept watch from tall towers built near the gates.

But when Vlad returned home, he was met with infuriating news. While he was away, his half brother Alexander Aldea had seized the throne of Wallachia. Vlad had the support of the emperor. But without soldiers to back it up, Sigismund's promise meant nothing.

Vlad settled in and began to plan. He built an alliance with neighboring Moldavia by arranging a new marriage for himself with a Moldavian princess. Young Vlad's mother, most likely, was forced to leave the family. With his new wife, the elder Vlad slowly began to raise an army.

Little Vlad, meanwhile, began his education. With his older brother, Mircea, he learned to dress and speak like a prince. He learned that his royal birth gave him the right to give orders to children from other families in town.

Vlad was barely more than a toddler when he began to train for a life of warfare. By five, he probably rode a horse bareback. He trapped rabbits and shot at eagles with a slingshot. Most likely, he learned to aim a bow and arrow.

Soon he took the name that would long outlive him. After joining the Order of the Dragon, Vlad's father became known as Vlad Dracul. *Dracul* meant "dragon" in Romanian. The younger Vlad became Dracula, or "little dragon."

But the word *dracula* had another meaning, as well. At the time, it's possible that no one thought much of it. But later writers, looking back on Vlad's life, thought it fit the prince well, for *dracula* also meant "little devil."

THE THREE EMPIRES

FOR CENTURIES BEFORE VLAD'S BIRTH, Europe had been divided into two empires. The Holy Roman Empire extended over much of western Europe. The Byzantine Empire stretched from eastern Europe into the western part of Asia.

The leaders of the Holy Roman Empire all worshipped in the Roman Catholic faith.

In the Byzantine Empire, the leaders followed another form of Christianity. They were called Orthodox Christians.

Vlad himself was divided. Like his father, he allied himself with the Holy Roman Empire. But he considered himself an Orthodox Christian.

In the 1400s, the two Christian empires—the Byzantine Empire and the Holy Roman Empire—faced a new enemy. That enemy was the Ottoman Empire. Its Turkish rulers were Muslim. And they were expanding their influence fast. By the time of Vlad's birth, they had taken over much of the Byzantine Empire. Their power extended north to the Danube River—just to the south of Vlad's homeland of Wallachia.

Family Ties

Prince Dracul angers his allies—and YOUNG VLAD PAYS THE PRICE.

By 1436, VLAD'S FATHER, VLAD DRACUL, stood prepared to take the throne of Wallachia from his half brother, Alexander Aldea. He had an army of hired soldiers from nearby towns. They were joined by Moldavians from his wife's homeland. Vlad Dracul supplied his troops with small, handheld cannons. They were among the first firearms used in Europe.

In the winter of 1436, Dracul saw his opportunity. Alexander Aldea lay on his deathbed, weak and open to attack. Dracul left his sons at home and led his soldiers south across the Carpathians. When Dracul's small army arrived at Targoviste, Aldea was in no condition to resist. Dracul entered the city and declared himself Prince of Wallachia.

For young Vlad, this was the beginning of a new era. The family moved to Targoviste with Vlad's new

THE PRINCE OF WALLACHIA lived in the palace in the capital city of Targoviste. Shown here are the remains of that palace.

baby brother Radu. Their stone palace stood at the center of the walled city.

In the gloomy rooms of the palace, Vlad began his training to become a knight. He had an old boyar as a tutor. He studied languages so he could speak with allies and negotiate with enemies. He read literature.

He also learned the skills he would need on the battlefield. Young Vlad rode on horseback through forests and mountains. He learned to fight with a sword and lance. He practiced with axes, hammers, and daggers. His most important lessons, though, came from watching his father.

Loyalty meant nothing to Prince Dracul. He betrayed his friends and befriended his enemies. When his enemies became friends, he betrayed them, too. He would sacrifice anything to stay in power.

In fact, Vlad was soon to learn, his father would even sacrifice his own children.

As a Dragon knight, Dracul had promised to protect the Holy Roman Empire from the Turks.

But in 1437, Emperor Sigismund died. And the Turks were growing strong. They were pressing against Wallachia from the south and west.

Under these conditions, Dracul had no problem ignoring his vow. He signed a peace treaty with the Turks. In 1438, he helped his new allies invade neighboring Transylvania.

Then, Christian forces of the Holy Roman Empire began to rally. The new emperor pledged to protect what was left of the Byzantine Empire from the Turks. His secret weapon was a Hungarian leader named János Hunyadi. The emperor put Hunyadi in charge of military campaigns against the Turks. And Hunyadi gave the Christians new hope. Eventually, he became known as the White Knight.

In 1441, Hunyadi came to Targoviste. He asked Dracul to join a crusade, or holy war, against the Turks. Dracul wanted to side with the victors. And since it wasn't clear who had the best chance of winning, he tried to stay neutral.

JÁNOS HUNYADI, KNOWN AS THE WHITE KNIGHT,
was determined to save the Christian empires from the Ottoman
Turks.

The following year, the Turks launched another raid on Transylvania. Dracul simply stood by and let the Turks pass through.

Hunyadi was furious with Dracul for cooperating with the Turks. The White Knight fought bitterly to defend Transylvania—and won. Then he chased the Turks back through Wallachia. Along the way, he forced Dracul out of Targoviste.

The events that followed aren't exactly clear. But it appears as though Dracul fled to the Turks, who were not happy with him either. Perhaps blaming him for their defeat, they threw Dracul in prison. There, 300 miles from home, Dracul made a deal that would change young Vlad's life forever. The Turks agreed to return Dracul to the throne of Wallachia. In exchange, Dracul made a series of promises. He pledged not to go to war against the Turks. He agreed to pay a sum of money every year. He offered to send young Wallachian men to the Turks to be converted to Islam and trained as soldiers.

Dracul probably did not plan to honor any of these pledges. But he made one final promise that he was forced to keep. He gave up two of his own sons as hostages.

Vlad was 12 or 13 at the time. What did he think when he learned that his father had traded him away in a political deal? Was he angry? Was he terrified? Maybe he understood that princes had to pay a high price in exchange for power. Only a few years earlier, a Serbian leader had given up two sons to the Turks as well. Could it be that power was the only important thing in life? That could have been the harshest lesson of all.

In the middle of 1443, Dracul returned to Wallachia. Young Vlad and Radu left the castle in Targoviste. They traveled 700 miles into the heart of the Ottoman Empire. Their journey ended in a mountain town filled with strangers. They became prisoners in a gloomy fortress. Their father, once again, became prince of Wallachia.

CHAPTER 3

Hostage Crisis

Vlad grows up
AT THE MERCY OF THE TURKS.

VLAD AND RADU must have been terrified. They sat in a fortress many miles from home—a journey of several weeks on horseback. They heard nothing from their parents for months on end.

At first, the Turks probably treated them well. Guards moved them to the capital city of Adrianople, 500 miles closer to home. There, they lived at the court of Sultan Murad II, the head of the Ottoman Empire.

The sultan did not treat his hostages like ordinary prisoners. These were the sons of a prince.

He planned to one day send Vlad and Radu home to rule their countries.

The sultan had Vlad and Radu educated by Turkish tutors. The two Wallachian princes studied mathematics and philosophy. They read the Muslim holy book, the Koran. They studied languages. Vlad learned to speak and read perfectly in Turkish.

VLAD WAS JUST 12 OR 13 when his father traded him and his brother for his own freedom. The boys were taken here, to the city of Adrianople, hundreds of miles from home.

SULTAN MURAD II HELD VLAD and Radu captive for years.
As a prisoner, Vlad was tough and quick to anger. His tutors often
used a whip to keep him in line.

But Vlad and Radu knew they weren't there simply to get an education. The Turks could be ruthless if the hostages, or their families, did not behave. The two Serbian princes were proof of that fact. In the spring of 1441, the Turks had caught them sending secret messages to their father. The sultan had the boys blinded with hot irons.

The sultan's message to the Serbian leader was clear: Obey, or your children will pay. Vlad and Radu must have gotten the message. They knew that their lives depended on the behavior of their father.

Back in Wallachia, Vlad Dracul understood the situation too. But he had a problem. On the borders of the Holy Roman Empire, the holy war was alive and well. And Wallachia stood right in the middle of it. Dracul felt pressure to go to war with his sons' captors.

In 1444, the Holy Roman Empire's White Knight, János Hunyadi, organized another crusade against the Turks. Once again, he insisted that

Dracul join him. Hunyadi hoped to move down the Danube to the port of Varna. His goal was to push the Turks out of Europe once and for all.

Hunyadi met with Dracul on the way to battle. Dracul tried once again to satisfy both sides. He refused to go to war himself. Instead, he sent his oldest son, Mircea, with a small force of 4,000 men.

Mircea apparently fought well. Gunpowder was new in Europe at the time, and he put it to use. He surprised the citizens of Petretz by battering the city walls with cannon fire. Mircea forced his way in. Then he dealt ruthlessly with the survivors. He had 50 Turks thrown to their death from the walls.

Mircea's victory was a small one, though. At Varna, the crusade ended in disaster for the Christian forces. They were badly outnumbered by the Turks. The king of Poland led a force of cavalry into battle. The Turks killed him in hand-to-hand combat. They chopped off his head and raised it on a pole for all to see. Hunyadi himself barely escaped alive.

Vlad Dracul knew that his decision to send Mircea into battle against the Turks may have doomed Vlad and Radu. When Dracul was criticized for not giving more support to the Holy Roman Empire, he replied passionately. "Please understand that I have allowed my children to be butchered for the sake of the Christian cause," he said.

Vlad and Radu, however, had not been butchered. Murad II probably still thought he could use them to bring Dracul back as an ally.

The sultan was right. In 1446, he let Dracul know that his sons were still alive. The following year, Dracul signed another treaty with the Turks. At age 16, Vlad was about to get his freedom back.

CHAPTER 4

Free at Last

VLAD LOSES HIS FAMILY—and gains an opportunity.

AT THE END OF 1447, Vlad got news of a disaster at home. According to legend, a boyar friend of Dracul's arrived breathless in Adrianople after riding nonstop for five days. The boyar supposedly brought two precious gifts from Vlad's father. He handed over the sword and the medallion that Dracul had received when he became a dragon knight. Then the boyar told his story.

After the battle of Varna, Dracul's uneasy friendship with Hunyadi had fallen apart. Dracul and Mircea blamed Hunyadi for the military defeat. Mircea even called for the White Knight to be tried and executed.

Hunyadi survived the accusations. Then he began to plot against Dracul. He contacted Vladislav II of the Danesti clan. The Danestis had been rivals of Dracul's family for decades. Hunyadi met with Vladislav at his home in Brasov. With an army behind them, the two men crossed the Carpathians and marched on Targoviste.

Vlad and Mircea closed the city gates to keep Hunyadi out. But Vladislav had supporters among the boyars inside the city. The boyars rose up in revolt. They captured Mircea, tortured him, and buried him alive.

Dracul managed to escape. But Vladislav's supporters chased him down. They shot the prince of Wallachia dead in a marsh near the city of Bucharest.

In the eyes of the sultan, Dracul's death changed everything. He informed Vlad that he was no longer

NO ONE REALLY KNOWS what Vlad Dracul, the father of Vlad the Impaler, looked like. But many people believe that this is a painting of him. It was found during a restoration of the family's home in Sighisoara, Romania, in 1976.

a prisoner. Instead he would become an officer in the Turkish army. Apparently, Vlad had impressed the sultan. The young prisoner was stubborn and strong-willed. The sultan thought he would make a perfect replacement for his father.

Vlad's reaction to the sudden rush of events has been lost to history. He had just lost his father and his brother. It's not clear what happened to his stepmother. The news must have come as a tremendous shock. Then again, by now, he may have come to expect the worst.

According to legend, Vlad swore to revenge his father's murder. It's easy to imagine his eyes narrowing in determination. With his father and brother gone, he now had a chance to take power for himself.

PART 2

Becoming Prince

CHAPTER 5

Prince for a Day

Vlad's first taste of power is sweet—
BUT VERY SHORT.

FOR FOUR YEARS, THE TURKS had been Vlad's prison guards. Suddenly, they became his allies. Murad II wanted to help Vlad take control of Wallachia. Together, they watched and waited for the right time.

In 1448, that time came. In September, Hunyadi launched another crusade against the Turks. He moved south across Wallachia. Vladislav II joined him with 8,000 Wallachian soldiers. The combined Christian force crossed the Danube. They pushed deep into Turkish territory in Serbia, looting homes and burning fields as they marched.

IN 1448, HUNYADI LAUNCHED AN ATTACK against the Turks. His army included Poles, Romanians, Hungarians, Serbs, and men from other areas. This illustration of Hungarian soldiers was created a few hundred years after Hunyadi's crusades.

Turkish spies told the sultan about Hunyadi's plans. The Turks surprised the Christian army at Kosovo Polje ("the field of blackbirds"). For three days in October, the Turks battled Hunyadi's army.

While Hunyadi and Vladislav fought, Vlad saw his chance to reclaim Wallachia. With a small army of Turkish horsemen, Vlad sneaked north toward

Targoviste. He entered the deserted city without a fight and declared himself prince.

Meanwhile, 250 miles to the southwest at Kosovo, the Turks crushed the Christian army. Hunyadi and Vladislav retreated with their troops in chaos.

The Turkish soldiers then stopped to bury their dead. They spent three days digging graves. Then the sultan ordered tables set up on the battlefield. The Turks had a feast among the bodies of the Hungarian soldiers.

While the Turks feasted, Hunyadi and Vladislav managed to save the remains of their army. Vladislav marched his troops to Wallachia to take his country back. He attacked Vlad and his army of Turkish soldiers. The battle was over almost before it started. Vladislav sent his young rival running back to Adrianople.

At 17, Vlad was on the run without a family or a home. He had been prince of Wallachia for less than two months.

CHAPTER 6

On the Run

VLAD GOES IN SEARCH OF A
way back to Wallachia.

At 18, VLAD FACED A CHOICE. Should he side with the Turks or return to the Christian world? If he stayed in Adrianople, he would urge the sultan to retake Wallachia and place him on the throne once and for all.

That may have seemed like Vlad's best hope. Hunyadi had been fighting the Turks for years without gaining ground. And the Turks had Constantinople surrounded. The city couldn't possibly hold out for long. When it fell, the Byzantine Empire would go with it. The Turkish navy would have free passage

47

from the Black Sea through to the Aegean. Ottoman troops would be free to invade Western Europe with all their strength. If Vlad stayed, he could become a prince in the ever-expanding Ottoman Empire.

But Vlad had other ideas. He may have felt pulled by his father's dragon oath. The Holy Roman Empire was the center of Christianity in the world. Maybe Vlad wasn't ready to turn his back on other Christians. Or maybe he had more selfish reasons to leave. Sultan Murad II could have lost confidence in him by now. Radu was coming of age. Perhaps Murad had chosen Radu over Vlad as the next ruler of Wallachia.

Vlad decided to set out on his own. Besides Radu, Vlad had few close relatives left in the world. Nearly two decades earlier, when Vlad's father needed allies, he had married into the ruling family of Moldavia. Now, the Moldavians were the closest thing Vlad had to family. Late in 1449, he went to find them.

Vlad settled in Suceava, Moldavia's capital city. It was now ruled by Bogdan II, Vlad's uncle by marriage.

Vlad made friends with Bogdan's son Stephen. The two cousins studied together. In 1450, they fought side by side in battle. They probably pledged their support to each other in future wars. Stephen may have promised to help Vlad return to Wallachia.

Then, Vlad's world was upset again. In October 1451, Prince Bogdan was assassinated. The assassin took over the throne of Moldavia.

Vlad and Stephen ran for their lives. They fled west to Transylvania—right into the hands of Hunyadi.

For at least a year, Vlad bounced around Transylvania. He tried to stay one step ahead of Hunyadi. By February 1452, he was hiding in the city of Brasov. Hunyadi told the city leaders to kick him out. "It is better that you capture him and chase him out of the country," he wrote. Not long after, Vlad escaped an assassin in the city of Sibiu.

Eventually, Hunyadi had a change of heart. He had lost faith in his Wallachian ally, Vladislav II.

The Wallachian leader had been negotiating with the Turkish sultan. Hunyadi felt he could no longer trust Vladislav to defend the borders against the Turks. So he turned to Vlad.

Vlad went to see Hunyadi in the Hungarian leader's mountain fortress. It must have been a tense

VLAD MET WITH HUNYADI HERE, in Hunyadi's mountain fortress, in what is now Romania. The meeting took place in 1452, five years after allies of Hunyadi killed Vlad's father.

meeting. Hunyadi, after all, was partly to blame for the death of Vlad's father and brother. And Vlad had close ties to Hunyadi's archenemies, the Turks.

No one knows what was said inside the fortress. But the two men decided to trust each other, at least for a time. Vlad had little choice. He was a man without a country. He needed Hunyadi's support. And Hunyadi needed Vlad as well. His spies had warned him that the Turks were preparing the final attack on Constantinople. Hunyadi wanted help defending the empire. And Vlad knew more about the enemy than anyone.

Hunyadi placed Vlad in charge of the southern border. He sent Vlad back to the city of Sibiu. Vlad made a home there, just 50 miles from his birthplace of Sighisoara. His job was much like the one his father had held 20 years earlier. Vlad was to defend the southern border of the empire against invasion from the Turks. With that job came an understanding. When the time came, Hunyadi would help Vlad become prince of Wallachia.

CONSTANTINOPLE

FOR A THOUSAND YEARS, CONSTANTINOPLE WAS THE JEWEL OF THE BYZANTINE EMPIRE. Perched above the Bosporus Strait, it occupied a vital strategic position. It guarded the narrow land passage from Asia to Europe and the all-important trade route from the Black Sea to the Mediterranean.

The city's beautiful domed churches and huge palaces were spread across seven hills. Since the early 400s, they had been guarded by 40-foot-tall walls, three layers deep. Until the invention of gunpowder, the walls were considered impossible to penetrate.

During the Middle Ages, Constantinople was among the largest, wealthiest cities in Europe. At its peak around the year 1000, it was home to a million people. Visitors marveled at its beauty. A 14th-century traveler from Russia was left breathless by the sight of the city's main cathedral. "As for St. Sophia," he wrote, "the human mind can neither tell it nor make description of it."

By that time, however, the city had already fallen from the height of its power. Thousands of people had moved away. And the Turks were closing in.

THIS WOODCUT OF CONSTANTINOPLE shows the city before the Turks were threatening to overtake it. As you can see, Constantinople was protected by layers of high walls.

A Light Goes Out

THE TURKS CLOSE IN
on the final outpost of a
thousand-year-old empire.

DURING THE SPRING OF 1453, Vlad must have anxiously followed the news from Constantinople. And the news did not sound good. Hunyadi had sent ambassadors to the Byzantine capital. The Hungarian warrior was the city's last hope. But before long, he called his men home. Hunyadi decided he couldn't save Constantinople.

The Ottomans had a new, more aggressive, leader. Murad II had died, and his son Mohammed had

MOHAMMED II BECAME SULTAN OF THE OTTOMAN EMPIRE after the death of his father, Murad II. Mohammed was determined to conquer Constantinople.

replaced him. The new sultan made no attempt to hide his intentions. Shortly after his father's death, he began to cut off Constantinople from outside help. The city sat on the Bosporus Strait, a thin line of water connecting the Black Sea with the Sea of Marmara. Mohammed built a huge fortress on the western shore of the Bosporus, at the narrowest part of the strait. He closed the waterway to any ship that refused to pay a fee. The fortress soon became known as "Cutthroat Castle."

The sultan also hired gun makers to build cannons for the Turks. The biggest of these monster guns fired metal balls weighing 600 pounds. It took 15 pairs of oxen to move it from place to place.

In Constantinople, the mood was grim. The city had 14 miles of walls to defend with an army of just 20,000. In the spring, people began to see signs of doom. A strange red glow supposedly lit the cathedral of St. Sophia from top to bottom. Some thought it came from the Turkish campfires surrounding the city. Others said it was Hunyadi, coming to save Constantinople. The sun nearly disappeared one day in an eclipse. Relentless rains brought flood waters into the streets. A dense fog settled in. Some people said God was leaving the city and didn't want people to see Him go.

THE MAIN CATHEDRAL IN CONSTANTINOPLE was
St. Sophia. In the final days of the Byzantine Empire, observers
swore that a strange red glow surrounded this building.

After months of waiting, the battle began in May.
More than 100,000 Turkish troops massed outside the
gates of Constantinople. Day after day, cannonballs
battered the gates of the city. A fleet of 100 ships shot
at the walls facing the sea.

The final assault came on May 29. Line after
line of soldiers stormed through the holes blasted

by the cannons. The leader of the Byzantine Empire, Emperor Constantine XI, came down from his throne. He fought in the streets with the troops of Constantinople. The last Byzantine emperor was killed by an unknown Turkish soldier. In a matter of days, Constantinople had fallen.

News of the conquest spread slowly around Europe. Many Christians listened in horror, as though the end of the world had arrived. The royal courts of France and England went into mourning. Bells rang in Russian churches to honor the Christians who had died in the battle. Pope Nicholas V insisted that the "light of Christianity" had gone out. "We shall not see it again in our lifetime," he said.

The reports that reached Vlad sounded just as gloomy. A Romanian bishop named Samuil escaped Constantinople and fled to Wallachia. He sent a letter off to the mayor of Sibiu, where Vlad watched over the borders. The next target for the Turkish army, Samuil said, was the great fortress of Belgrade. On the way there, they were sure to overrrun Sibiu. "The Turks," Samuil warned, "will eventually subdue all of Christianity if God will allow it."

Hunyadi, for one, was determined not to allow it.

WHEN THE OTTOMAN TURKS CONQUERED CONSTANTINOPLE IN 1453, the Byzantine Empire was brought to an end. Leaders of the Holy Roman Empire feared that their empire was next.

CHAPTER 8

Power to the Prince

Vlad comes HOME AT LAST.

FOR THREE YEARS after the fall of Constantinople, Hunyadi and Vlad prepared for battle. They hired soldiers and bought weapons. They were determined to defend Belgrade at all costs.

The Serbian city stood on a hill guarding the Danube. If it fell, it would leave a river route open to western Europe. Walls three layers thick protected its inner city. But the city kept only a force of 5,000 men. If the Turks attacked, Belgrade would need help.

By the winter of 1455, Vlad and Hunyadi knew that an attack was coming. Sultan Mohammed had a force of 90,000 men at Adrianople. He had a fleet of 60 ships where the Danube poured into the Black Sea, waiting to sail upriver toward Belgrade.

In June of 1456, the attack began. The huge Turkish army moved slowly up the Danube. Oxen pulled 27

THE FORTRESS AT BELGRADE HAD PROTECTED the city from invaders for more than 1,000 years. But the Turks were determined to blow it open.

enormous cannons. The fleet of ships followed on the river.

As the Turks closed in on Belgrade, Hunyadi tried to pull together allies to defend Belgrade. He and a 70-year-old friar named John of Capistrano led 16,000 men toward the city. Vlad led another force south toward Wallachia. His job was to keep the Wallachian prince,

THE WARRIOR, JÁNOS HUNYADI (in the front), and the friar, John Capistrano (holding the cross), led the Hungarian peasants against the Turkish army at Belgrade.

Vladislav II, from helping the Turks. If possible, he would get rid of Vladislav and claim Wallachia for himself.

The Turks surrounded Belgrade, just as they had done at Constantinople. They blasted their way through the outer walls. On July 21, Sultan Mohammed ordered the final attack. Thousands of Turks closed in on the inner city.

But Hunyadi and John of Capistrano were there to meet them. John's men were mostly poor farmers. They fought with pitchforks, clubs, and whatever else they could find. Together with Hunyadi's Hungarian soldiers, they held off the Turks.

When the battle was over, Belgrade was safe. The Turks had lost 24,000 men. Many Christians called it a "miracle." The new pope, Eugenius IV, said it was the "happiest event of my life."

Meanwhile, in July, Vlad emerged from the Carpathians. With his small force of hired soldiers, he moved toward Targoviste. While Hunyadi was fighting the Turks, Vlad led his men into battle against Vladislav II.

Nearly 10 years after his father's death, Vlad got his revenge. Vladislav died in hand-to-hand combat on the battlefield. Vlad may well have been the person who killed him.

Sometime in August of 1456, Vlad entered Targoviste. He was still in his twenties. But he had waited a long time for this moment. Like his father before him, he declared himself prince of Wallachia.

By the time the news reached Transylvania, Hunyadi was not around to hear it. A deadly plague had marched up the Danube with the Turks. Rats on the Turkish ships probably spread the disease as the fleet moved west. Hunyadi, middle-aged by now, was in no shape to resist the plague. He got sick and died on August 11.

As far as we know, Vlad was in fine health. Targoviste, however, was emptying out around him. The boyars of the city fled into the mountains to escape the plague. Eventually, they returned to begin life under their new prince. Vlad made many of them wish they had never come back.

BLACK DEATH

DURING VLAD'S TIME, AN INVISIBLE KILLER TERRORIZED EUROPE. It was deadlier than the cruelest tyrant. The killer was a disease called the bubonic plague. It arrived in the form of a germ carried by fleas. The fleas made their home on the backs of rats. The rats hopped aboard seagoing ships. They carried their deadly cargo to all corners of the known world.

The plague struck humans with great violence. Victims came down with a high fever. Their limbs ached. Then they vomited blood. Lumps, or "buboes," swelled up in their neck, armpits, or groin. The lumps turned dark in color, giving the disease its nickname, "Black Death." Finally, the lumps burst and the victim died. The whole process, from the onset of the disease to death, took three or four days.

When the plague first hit Europe in 1348, it stayed for five years. During that time it killed 25 million people. Just like that, one-third of Europe's population was gone.

A VICTIM of the Black Death

Vlad the Impaler in Pictures

THE PICTURE OF CRUELTY

Vlad was born in a small town in Transylvania called Sighisoara. He was know as *Dracula*, or "little dragon." The name also meant "little devil."

A VIOLENT CHILDHOOD

Vlad was born in this house. As a boy, he probably spent a lot of time outdoors. He learned to fight with a sword and a lance. He also practiced with axes, hammers, and daggers.

A FATHER'S BETRAYAL

Vlad Dracul, Vlad's father, was captured by the Turks when Vlad was a young boy. To gain his freedom, Vlad Dracul agreed to hand over his sons Vlad and Radu to this man, Sultan Murad II.

FEAR OF DEATH

Vlad and Radu were imprisoned for four years in the city of Adrianople. They received a good education there, but they knew that at any moment, they could be killed.

END OF AN ERA

When the Ottoman Turks conquered
Constantinople in 1453, the Byzantine
Empire came to an end.

THE WHITE KNIGHT

Leaders from the Holy Roman Empire hoped
that this man, János Hunyadi, would save
western Europe from the Ottoman Turks. In
1452, Vlad had met with Hunyadi and pledged—
reluctantly—to help him.

OBSESSED BY THE THRONE

Throughout his life, Vlad's primary goal was to be the prince of Wallachia and to live in the palace at Targoviste, the capital of the country. Pictured here is a restoration of the original building.

WAR IN THE MOUNTAINS

Many of the battles that Vlad fought with Hunyadi took place in what is now the country of Romania, an area marked by steep mountains, sharp ragged cliffs, and unforgiving terrain.

PRINCE OF WALLACHIA

Three times Vlad became prince of Wallachia, and three times he was chased from his country. This sculpture shows him just after he took the throne for the first time.

A TASTE FOR BLOOD

Stories about Vlad's cruelty spread throughout Europe. According to one tale, after he raided a town in 1459 and impaled everyone he could find, he sat down in the midst of the corpses and enjoyed a meal.

A CASTLE BUILT ON CORPSES

Further evidence of Vlad's cruelty was the Poenari Fortress. In 1457, he killed most of the leaders in Wallachia. Then he forced the survivors to build a castle for him in the mountains—until they literally dropped dead of hunger and exhaustion.

THE MONSTER IS IMPRISONED

Vlad's brother Radu, backed by the people of Wallachia, chased Vlad from the country. Vlad appealed to King Matthias Corvinus for protection. Instead, Corvinus imprisoned him here, in Solomon's Tower.

THE HEAD OF DRACULA

Vlad Dracula was killed in 1476. His headless body was later found in a marsh. This sculpture is in Vlad's hometown of Sighisoara, in what is now Romania.

GRAVE OF DRACULA

Dracula's body (minus the head) is said to lie here, in the chapel at the Snagov monastery in the middle of a lake.

VAMPIRES ATTACK!

There have been vampire legends for hundreds of years. In these tales, creatures come back from death as bats and feast on the blood of their victims. But how did Vlad the Impaler become Dracula the vampire?

VLAD DRACULA BECOMES UNDEAD

An Irish writer named Bram Stoker (above) wrote the novel that connected these legends to the bloodthirsty Vlad the Impaler, also known as Vlad Dracula. It's likely that Stoker didn't know much about the prince, but Stoker borrowed his name. The author also placed his vampire in Transylvania, Vlad's birthplace.

BRAM STOKER'S DRACULA

Stoker's novel was *Dracula*, published in 1897. In this book, a young man named Jonathan Harker visits the strange Count Dracula in Transylvania. Dracula follows Harker back to England and tries to suck the life from Harker's fiancée. (Shown here is a French version of the book.)

DRACULA ON THE SILVER SCREEN

Since the publication of Stoker's novel, *Dracula* has been made into countless films. One of the first was *Nosferatu: A Symphony of Terror*, released in 1922. Filmgoers never heard Dracula's victims scream; the film was silent.

THE LEGEND LIVES ON

Dracula got a new face in this 1992 film, *Bram Stoker's Dracula*. Winona Ryder played Harker's fiancée, and Gary Oldman played Dracula.

AM DRACULA. I BID YOU WELCOME."

e of the most famous Dracula movies was the 1931 version with
r Bela Lugosi. Lugosi was an immigrant from Romania—the
ntry in which Transylvania is now located.

PART 3

The Impaler Rules

CHAPTER 9

Blood of the Boyars

Vlad begins his reign as prince with
A BRUTAL SHOW OF POWER.

FINALLY, VLAD RULED his own land again.
About half a million people fell under his control.
Before long, they would fear their own prince more
than they feared the Turks.

Vlad moved into the stone castle in Targoviste,
where he had spent much of his childhood. Right
away, he tried to make allies. He signed treaties with
the Transylvanian cities of Sibiu and Brasov. He also

VLAD GREETED VISITORS at the castle of Targoviste. They
were no doubt impressed by the castle's splendor—
and by Vlad's charm.

pledged his loyalty to the king of nearby Hungary. In 1457, he raised an army of 6,000 men to help his cousin Stephen. With the Wallachian troops, Stephen invaded Moldavia. He took the country back from his father's assassin.

In Adrianople, Sultan Mohammed watched Vlad's dealings with interest. Before long, he sent ambassadors to Wallachia. They demanded that Vlad pay a yearly tax of 2,000 gold pieces. They also insisted that Vlad let Turkish soldiers pass through on raids into Transylvania. Vlad agreed, even though he had promised his protection to the people of Brasov and Sibiu.

Vlad no doubt had the abililty to impress foreign visitors. He was well educated. He spoke many languages. At least at the beginning of his reign, he seemed ready to agree to anything.

To his rivals at home, he showed a very different face—the face of a monster. The boyars quickly came to know it well. For years, these wealthy landowners had shared power with the princes of Wallachia. A boyar council met in Targoviste to help the prince govern. The council helped make laws. It approved or rejected the decisions of the prince. In 1457, many of the Wallachian boyars still supported Vladislav II and his Danesti clan. They were suspicious of Vlad—and for good reason.

Vlad had no desire to share power with the boyars. He didn't trust them. And he believed firmly that a prince should have to answer to no one. His solution was to terrorize the boyars into obeying him.

Wallachians got their first taste of this policy during the Easter Massacre of 1457. Terror must have settled over Targoviste as Vlad's guards impaled one boyar after another. When the executioners finished their bloody work, Vlad was still not done. He had his guards round up the younger boyars of the city. Women and children were taken as well as men. The guards put the prisoners in chains and marched them 50 miles up the Arges River into the mountains.

After climbing for two days, the exhausted

boyars arrived at a high mountain rock. On top of the rock stood the ruins of an old castle. Vlad put his prisoners to work rebuilding it. Every day they formed a human chain stretching up the steep cliffs. At the bottom, prisoners slaved over hot ovens. They made bricks and passed them up the line to the castle. It was backbreaking work in dangerous terrain. Eventually, Castle Dracula, also called the Poenari Fortress, took shape. No one knows how many prisoners died building it.

VLAD LITERALLY WORKED THE BOYARS TO DEATH
building the Castle Dracula, also known as the Poenari Fortress.

During the first few years of Vlad's reign, the boyars nearly disappeared from Wallachia. Some were executed. Others fled to Transylvania. Still more escaped to Turkey, where Radu had become an officer in the Turkish army.

The attacks on the boyars were sadistic and cruel. But they weren't random. Vlad had a plan for Wallachia. He had goals for his country. And terror was the way he achieved them.

CHAPTER 10

Ruling With an Iron Stake

VLAD MAKES HIS POINT:
There will be law and order
throughout the land.

WITH THE EASTER MASSACRE, Vlad got rid of his most powerful enemies. Now he turned to another task. In the violent world around him, princes didn't last long. Vlad was determined to stay in power. He wanted a stable country where people obeyed the law. He demanded total loyalty from his subjects. His strategy was to keep them all in a constant state of terror.

A half century later, the Italian writer Niccolò Machiavelli produced a widely read book of advice for princes. In it, he wrote a famous line, "It is safer

THIS SCULPTURE OF VLAD, still on display in Tarogviste, shows him victorious after he has taken the throne of Wallachia.

to be feared than loved." Vlad could not have said it better himself.

To enforce his reign of terror, Vlad reorganized Wallachia's military forces. He created a new group of officers called the *viteji*. They would lead the army in battle against foreign invasions.

He also set up a national guard, called the *sluji*. He used the *sluji* as a police force. They guarded Vlad's castles and cracked down on his political enemies. They also helped chase down lawbreakers.

Anyone convicted of a crime was handed over to a third new group of soldiers, the *armasi*. The *armasi* served as Vlad's executioners. The tools of their trade were chains, axes, swords and, most importantly, stakes.

Many of Vlad's new recruits came from the lower classes. With the boyars out of the way, Vlad needed allies. He found them among the peasants and craftsmen of Wallachia. In time, they would actually see Vlad as their protector. He gave them positions of importance at his court. He reduced taxes for peasants. He took land from boyar estates and gave it to poor families. He made sure that rich people could no longer buy their way out of punishment for a crime.

But Vlad was hardly a friend of the poor. He hated anyone who relied on others for support. According to legend, one day he rounded up the homeless and the beggars, the blind, and the lame. He invited them to Targoviste for a feast, just as he had invited the boyars on Easter Sunday. Vlad's ragged guests gathered in a mansion to eat and drink. When they were all drunk, Vlad locked them in and set the building on fire. Not a single guest escaped alive.

Not surprisingly, Vlad was also ruthless with thieves. People could be impaled for stealing a few pieces of gold. According to legend, Vlad loved to test his subjects. He supposedly kept a gold cup next to a well near his castle. No one ever dared to steal it.

According to another story, an Italian merchant asked Vlad for shelter one night. Vlad took the merchant in, but had him leave his possessions outside. In the morning, the man's gold was gone. Vlad told the merchant not to worry; he would catch the thief. In the meantime, he secretly replaced the gold—with one extra coin. When the merchant found the gold, he was overjoyed. He reported the news to Vlad, and told him about the extra coin. Vlad congratulated the merchant. If he had lied about the extra coin, Vlad said, he would have been impaled along with the thief.

Vlad even kept a close eye on people's private behavior. Married people who had affairs were cruelly punished. They could have body parts cut off or be skinned alive. Under Vlad, even laziness became a crime. According to one story, he met a peasant whose clothes were sewn in a sloppy way. Vlad assumed the man's wife was not doing her job. He had the poor woman impaled on the spot.

Law and order had come to Wallachia. The cost: Tens of thousands of lives—and constant terror.

CHAPTER 11

Raids of Terror

VLAD TURNS HIS WRATH on two cities full of hardworking Germans.

VLAD'S CRUELTY DID NOT FRIGHTEN all of his enemies into obeying him. It did, however, chase them outside the borders of Wallachia. Several of Vlad's rivals settled just across the Carpathians in Transylvania. Vladislav II's brother Dan III made his home near Brasov. Vlad's own half brother, a man called Vlad the Monk, hid near Sibiu. They settled in and waited for a chance to take over Wallachia.

Vlad was determined not to let them.

Vlad started off on good terms with the people of Brasov and Sibiu. The two cities and their surrounding towns had a large population of German merchants and craftsmen. The Germans were important to the Wallachian economy. They crafted cloth and shoes, jewelry and clocks. Their metalworkers made the latest weapons. The merchants brought their goods to Wallachia to trade in cities like Targoviste.

When Vlad first became prince, he signed a treaty with Brasov and Sibiu. He let the German merchants trade freely in Wallachia. He promised the cities protection from the Turks. Both sides agreed not to support the political enemies of the other.

The friendship didn't last long.

In 1457, Germans along the border between Wallachia and Transylvania revolted against the relatives of János Hunyadi, who ruled Transylvania. Vlad, who still supported the Hunyadis, helped put down the rebellion. Then he began to crack down on the Germans. He told his guards to stop German merchants at the border.

He ordered their carts unpacked. Then he allowed Wallachian merchants to buy the goods at low prices.

When the Germans tried to avoid the border guards, Vlad took revenge. He rode into the Sibiu region with a small army of horsemen. They swept through villages waving torches. Hundreds of helpless townspeople were burned alive in their homes.

Vlad made a brief attempt to negotiate with the German cities. He offered to make peace if the leaders of Sibiu and Brasov would hand over Vlad the Monk and Vladislav's brother Dan III. Vlad got no response.

In the spring of 1458, he set out to punish the German cities. He swept across the mountains and tore through the countryside in anger. He destroyed three towns near Sibiu, where Vlad the Monk's supporters lived. Then he turned toward Brasov. Few people escaped alive. Vlad supposedly killed everyone in the village of Bod. In nearby Talmes, according to a German account, he had the people "hacked to pieces like cabbage." He took a few prisoners on the raid. They were all marched back to Targoviste and impaled.

By this time, Germans were fleeing Vlad's horsemen by the hundreds. They escaped west to Austria and other parts of the Holy Roman Empire. They told their stories to anyone who would listen. Several German monks wrote about the terror Vlad spread through the German cities. The stories may be exaggerated. But if they are even close to the truth, they show Vlad to be one of the cruelest tyrants in history.

According to the German accounts, Vlad caught 600 merchants sneaking into Wallachia. He placed them in huge pots with their heads sticking through holes in the lids. Then he had them boiled alive. On another occasion he supposedly rounded up 400 German boys who came to Wallachia to learn the language. Dracula accused them of spying. As punishment, he locked them in a room and burned them all to death.

In the winter of 1459, Vlad launched his most terrifying raid. This time, he went in search of Dan III.

ACCORDING TO LEGEND, AFTER VLAD RAIDED A TOWN
and impaled the residents, he sat down in the midst of the corpses
and enjoyed a meal.

Outside of Brasov, he burned a town and its church. After impaling everyone he could find, he sat down among the corpses and ate a meal. One German monk claimed that Vlad dipped his bread in the blood of his victims.

Dan III finally decided it was time to strike back. He sent a message to the people of Brasov. Vlad was a "cruel tyrant" who tortured and killed people "aimlessly," he said. Then Dan asked anyone who had "lost a dear one" in the fighting to come to his support.

In March 1460, Dan III led an army into Wallachia. Near the border he ran into Vlad's horsemen. Dan III didn't stand a chance. All but seven of his men were captured or killed. Dan himself met a terrible fate. Vlad staged a funeral for him while Dan watched. Then he made Dan dig his own grave. Finally, Vlad chopped off his rival's head and tossed him in the grave.

Vlad made one final raid on the German cities in search of Vlad the Monk. He never found his half brother. But in October 1460 he grew tired of looking. Vlad and his enemies in Transylvania finally agreed to a truce. The Germans, no doubt, had seen enough blood.

For his part, Vlad had another enemy to worry about. His unsteady peace with the Turks was beginning to fall apart.

CHAPTER 12

Taking It to the Turks

VLAD HAS A SURPRISE
for the sultan.

SINCE THEIR DEFEAT AT BELGRADE IN 1456, the Turks had been quiet. They strengthened their fortresses along the Danube. And they waited.

In 1460, they began to move again. They captured a town just to the east of Belgrade. They also began to put pressure on Vlad.

During the years of war with the German cities, Vlad had ignored his treaty with the Turks. Sultan

Mohammed II now demanded 10,000 gold pieces a year from Wallachia. He wanted 500 Wallachians for his army. And he expected Vlad to come to Constantinople to kiss the hem of his gown.

It's hard to imagine Vlad kissing anyone's gown. He demanded respect from all foreigners—and was prepared to do anything to get it. According to one story, Vlad once received several of the sultan's ambassadors. The Turks bowed in greeting when they arrived. But they failed to take their turbans off their heads. It was their custom to keep their heads covered, they said. Vlad replied that he would be happy to help them follow their customs. He then had his guards nail the turbans to their heads.

In November 1461, Vlad was in a more friendly mood. He wrote to Mohammed II to explain why he hadn't honored the treaty with the Turks. He could not afford to pay the tax, he claimed. The war with the Germans had been too expensive. Instead, he promised to send horses and young men for the Turkish army.

Most likely, Vlad was stalling for time. He believed the Turks were planning to invade Wallachia. Vlad's brother Radu still lived with the Turks. Perhaps the sultan was just waiting for a chance to replace Vlad with Radu. The thought must have made Vlad furious. He decided he would be the one to strike first.

That winter, Sultan Mohammed invited Vlad to a meeting in the city of Giurgiu, a city controlled by the Turks. Vlad agreed to go, but he sensed a plot. He was convinced that the sultan wanted to seize him and bring him back to Constantinople.

Vlad made a plan of his own. He set off for Giurgiu with a small group of men. He ordered a large force of cavalry to follow behind, where they wouldn't be seen by the Turks. When he arrived at Giurgiu, Vlad supposedly disguised himself as a Turk. The Turkish guards opened the gate, and Vlad's men stormed in. They killed Giurgiu's defenders, looted the city, and burned the fortress to the ground.

Vlad then launched a vicious attack against the Turks. He led his cavalry on a rampage, 500 miles down the Danube to the Black Sea. For two weeks his horsemen swept through Turkish-controlled Bulgaria. In town after town they destroyed everything they could find. They ruined food supplies. They chopped the heads off of Turkish soldiers. They burned people

AFTER VLAD LAUNCHED HIS BRUTAL ATTACK ON THE TURKS, he sat down and wrote János Hunyadi's son, Matthias Corvinus, the new king of Hungary. Vlad was certain that Corvinus would send him backup.

in their homes. All the while, Vlad carefully counted his victims: 6,840 in Durostos, 6,414 in Giurgiu, 1,460 at Rahova, and so on.

When the killing was over, Vlad returned to Giurgiu. He must have been filled with the thrill of victory. He had just single-handedly launched a new crusade against the mighty Turks.

Now, he needed help.

Vlad sat down to let the Christian world know about his deeds. He started with János Hunyadi's son, Matthias Corvinus. Matthias was now king of Hungary. He had the power and the resources to send troops to Wallachia. Vlad wrote to Matthias on February 11, 1462. He described his raid along the Danube in detail. He bragged that he had killed 23,884 Turks and Bulgarians. To prove his point, Vlad sent along two bags of evidence. Inside were the heads, noses, and ears of dozens of victims.

Vlad brought his army back to Targoviste. Over the next three months, he tried desperately to get help. He told Matthias that if Wallachia fell to the Turks, Hungary would be next. He wrote to his cousin Stephen in Moldavia. He sent messengers to the Italians, the Armenians, and the Tatars. Everyone praised Vlad's courage against the Turks. But no one was willing to help.

Vlad had started a war. Now, he would have to finish it himself.

CHAPTER 13

No More at Stake

In the final battle, there are
NO ALLIES TO BE FOUND.

IN THE SPRING OF 1462, Sultan Mohammed
decided to launch a counterattack against Vlad. He
gathered the largest Turkish army since the capture
of Constantinople. He left Constantinople in May with
about 60,000 troops. The Turkish army marched up the
south bank of the Danube. Vlad's brother, Radu, backed
him up with a force of 4,000 Wallachian horsemen. A
fleet of ships escorted them up the river.

On the north side of the Danube, Vlad commanded
an army of 20,000 to 30,000. Most of his soldiers were

peasants. They carried axes, hammers, or swords. Some fought with bows and arrows. Many of the Wallachians wore vests of tough animal hide to protect against the swords of the Turks.

Vlad sent scouts to follow the progress of the Turkish troops. But in early June, the Turks took him by surprise. They crossed the river at the town of Turnu with 120 cannons. The Turks dug trenches and blasted the Wallachians with the big guns.

Outgunned and outnumbered, Vlad was forced to retreat north toward Targoviste. He ordered his soldiers to destroy everything in sight. They burned houses and crops. They poisoned the wells. They drove cattle away. They ate or ruined any food they could find. Peasants and boyars all escaped with the retreating army.

The Turks followed closely behind. In Vlad's path they found nothing but empty villages and scorched earth. There was nothing to eat or drink. Supposedly, the land was so hot that the soldiers could roast what

IN 1462, SULTAN MOHAMMED II gathered about 60,000 troops and attacked Vlad and his allies. The Turks, who had more weapons and more soldiers, forced Vlad and his men to retreat.

little meat they had on their shields. At night Vlad hammered at the Turks with hit-and-run attacks.

By the middle of June, the Turks neared Targoviste. Guards still manned the cannons in the capital city. But the Turks held the advantage. By one account, they had Vlad trapped in a dense forest.

Vlad was in trouble, and he knew it. On June 17, he launched a desperate night attack. Three hours after sundown, his men stormed the Turkish camp. They hacked and stabbed their way through the camp, looking for the Sultan Mohammed's tent. For several hours, a terrible battle raged. Vlad's men slaughtered thousands of Turks. But they never found the sultan. Just before dawn they gave up the attack. Vlad led his men back to their forest hideaway.

The attack had been a daring success. But Vlad was furious that he had failed to kill the sultan. According to one story, he turned his anger on his men. He rounded up all soldiers who had been wounded in the battle. He picked out the men with wounds in the

AFTER VLAD'S BUTCHERY, the beautiful countryside outside of Targoviste (shown here) was transformed into a horrifying scene— the forest of the impaled.

back and accused them of running away. He had each of them impaled on the spot.

But while Vlad butchered his own men, the sultan was already losing his courage. Just outside of Targoviste, he entered the "forest of the impaled." Vlad himself had arranged the scene. A hideous fence of stakes guarded the city gates. Rotting bodies drooped from the stakes. Corpses dangled from tree limbs. The smell of decaying flesh hung in the air. Some accounts insist that Vlad had left 20,000 bodies to greet the Turks.

The sultan decided he was done with the war. He retreated to the east. By July, he was back in Adrianople. Mohammed left Radu in charge of the war in Wallachia. And Vlad's brother finished what the sultan had started.

Radu sent out an appeal to the Wallachian people. He urged them to rise up and chase Vlad out of the country. You have "suffered long enough because of my brother," he said.

The Wallachian people responded. For six years they had lived in terror of Vlad. Thousands of people had been killed and tortured. In the previous month, huge stretches of farmland had been ruined. Peasants and boyars had been forced from their homes.

In a matter of weeks, the Wallachians deserted their prince. Vlad's boyar enemies were probably the first to go. Then peasants began to leave the army. They found Radu and joined his drive to become prince.

Vlad fought on through September. But he had no help at home or abroad. He had hoped for support from his cousin Stephen in Moldavia. But Stephen had actually attacked a Wallachian town on his border while Vlad was at war with the Turks. For months, Vlad had begged King Matthias of Hungary for aid. Matthias had promised to lead an army in Vlad's defense. But in October, the king and his troops were still nowhere near Wallachia.

Vlad was alone and on the run. Only a small group of bodyguards remained at his side. Winter began to fall over the Carpathians.

Vlad watched while his country slipped away into the hands of his brother. He had only his own cruelty to blame. In the fall, Radu declared himself prince of Wallachia. Then he chased the defeated tyrant into the snowy Carpathians.

PART 4

The Final Years

CHAPTER 14

Escape!

A DARING RIDE through the mountains leads Vlad into the hands of a friend—or so he thought.

LATE IN 1462, VLAD CLIMBED with his small group of followers to his castle on the Arges River. The bodies of the boyar slaves who built the castle probably laid buried nearby.

Vlad may have thought he was safe in his mountain hideaway. But Radu sent a force of Turkish soldiers up the Arges after his brother. The soldiers camped across the river and aimed their cannons at the castle. Dracula was surrounded.

The Turks planned their final attack for the following morning.

Romanians still tell stories about the events that followed. Supposedly a Wallachian slave in the Turkish army gave Vlad a warning. In the middle of the night, he attached a note to an arrow. He shot the arrow through a tiny window in the castle. The arrow hit a candle in the room and put out the flame. When Vlad's wife went to relight the candle she saw the warning note.

Vlad's wife refused to be captured alive. She threw herself off the castle into the riverbed far below. The place where she fell came to be known as the "Princess' River."

According to legend, Vlad followed a secret passageway down to the river. He sneaked away on horseback with his young son and 12 followers. Above them in the castle, Vlad's men fired cannons all night to distract the Turks. The guns startled the horse that carried Vlad's son. The horse ran off with Vlad's son clinging to it. His father did not stop to look for him.

RUNNING FOR THEIR LIVES, Vlad and his men struggled through the snowy Carpathians to seek help from Matthias Corvinus, King of Hungary.

Vlad still had one last hope. King Matthias was on his way to Brasov with an army. With fresh troops, Vlad could possibly force his way back into Targoviste and send Radu running back to the sultan.

The trip to Brasov was dangerous. Vlad and his small following made their way over steep cliffs covered in snow and ice. Finally, in November, he met Matthias in Brasov. Vlad must have hoped for a warm welcome. After all, he had driven the sultan back to Adrianople. In his view, he had kept the Turks away from Matthias's borders.

The Hungarian king didn't see it that way. He trapped Vlad at a nearby castle and had him arrested. He accused Vlad of secretly forming an alliance with the sultan. He also spread stories about Vlad's cruelty to his subjects at home. Then he declared his support for Vlad's brother, the new prince of Wallachia.

The king set off for the Hungarian capital of Buda. Guards carried Vlad along behind. After six years as ruler of Wallachia, the fearsome impaler was once again a prisoner.

CHAPTER 15

A Legacy of Cruelty

After years in prison,
Vlad comes back, only to
LOSE HIS HEAD ONE LAST TIME.

Not MUCH IS KNOWN about the next 12 years of Vlad's life. He spent some time in a Hungarian prison. Most likely he stayed in a fortress called Solomon's Tower, near the city of Buda.

Even in prison, Vlad found ways to satisfy his cruelty. According to a Russian account, he managed

VLAD HAD EXPECTED HIS OLD ALLY, MATTHIAS
CORVINUS, to protect him from his enemies. Instead, Corvinus
locked him up here, in Solomon's Tower. Vlad spent 12
years in this prison.

to capture birds and rodents. Then he tortured the
defenseless animals.

After a time, Matthias began to relax his hold over
Vlad. At some point, he offered Vlad a deal. Vlad had

to give up his Orthodox faith and become a Catholic. He would marry into the Hungarian royal family. In return, Matthias would free him and support his return to Wallachia.

It was a deal that Vlad could not refuse. He converted to Catholicism and got married. Vlad and his new wife moved into a large house in Pest, across the river from Buda. They had two children. And by 1475, Vlad was back in action again.

The Turks had taken over much of Bosnia, to the west of Serbia. They were closing in on Hungary. King Matthias needed Vlad's help. He reached out to Stephen and to Vlad. That summer, the three of them joined forces. They pledged to launch a crusade against the Turks.

At the beginning of 1476, the campaign began. Vlad and Matthias led 5,000 men toward Turkish positions in Bosnia. And Vlad was once again able to satisfy his taste for blood. A report on his cruelty made its way back to the Pope. According to the Pope's envoy, Vlad "tore the limbs off the Turkish prisoners and placed their parts on stakes."

When Vlad returned from battle, he set his eyes on his final goal. He wanted to rule Wallachia once again. In November, he got his chance. Stephen led a force of 15,000 into eastern Wallachia. Vlad led another 35,000 men down from Transylvania in the north.

By this time Radu had been replaced by an old rival of Vlad's, a man named Basarab Laiota. Basarab was there to meet Vlad at the border. The two armies fought fiercely. When the smoke cleared, each side had lost 10,000 men. Basarab fled to the east. Vlad pushed on to the south and entered Targoviste.

Home at last, Vlad declared himself prince of Wallachia. Stephen soon arrived with his Moldavian troops. It had been 25 years since the cousins first took an oath of friendship in Moldavia. Once again, Vlad pledged his support to Stephen until the end of his life.

It didn't take much to keep the promise. Within a month, Vlad was dead.

His last battle took place near Bucharest at the end of December. Vlad had pursued Basarab's forces there. Most likely he was killed by a Turkish assassin fighting with Basarab. The killer supposedly cut off Vlad's head. He took his prize back to Constantinople. The impaler's head was raised on a stake for all to see.

Soon after, some Wallachian monks found Vlad's headless corpse in a marsh. They brought his body to the Snagov monastery. The monastery sits on an island in the middle of a great lake. The monks buried the prince in a chapel, facing the altar of the church.

To this day, legend has it that Vlad's spirit haunts the island. According to folktales, a great wind blew up on the day Vlad was buried. It tore the chapel off its foundation and hurled it into the lake. Supposedly, you can still hear the bell ringing beneath the water.

Many people claim that Vlad had evil plans for the monastery. According to the story, he wanted to build a torture chamber there. He planned a room with a trapdoor cut into the floor. He would lure prisoners onto the trap door. Then he would send them plunging onto stakes positioned just below.

It's a plan that could easily have come from the mind of this cruel prince. Yet in a final twist of fate, Vlad was trapped forever in his own prison.

DRACULA'S HEADLESS BODY MAY LIE HERE, in the chapel at the Snagov monastery, in the middle of a lake.

THIS STATUE OF VLAD is in Bucharest,
in what is now Romania.

Wicked?

Exactly how much damage did Vlad Dracula do during his lifetime? He ruled Wallachia for just seven years. It's hard to say how many victims he claimed. By one account, he murdered 100,000 people. If that were true, he killed off one-fifth the population of Wallachia. Those numbers would make him nearly as deadly as the Black Death. In fact, the number is probably closer to 40,000. If so, he killed about one out of every 12 Wallachians. That's still enough to place him among the cruelest rulers in history.

Stories of Vlad's cruelty spread quickly, while he was still alive and after his death. His enemies made sure of that. The German monks who escaped Vlad's raids had their tales written down. The stories were printed into booklets and sold as popular reading. Publishers gave the booklets titles like, "The Frightening and Truly Extraordinary Story of a Wicked Blood-drinking Tyrant Called Prince Dracula."

Some of them came with shocking pictures. The cover of one displayed a woodcut of Vlad eating a meal surrounded by impaled victims.

The German stories showed Vlad as a bloodthirsty tyrant. But not everyone saw him that way. To many people in Romania, Vlad was a hero. His defenders say that Vlad was the strong leader that Wallachia needed. He stamped out crime in the countryside and the cities. He crushed the boyars, who were taking advantage of the peasantry. He stood up to the Turks when the rest of Europe did not.

Which is the real Vlad Dracula? It's certainly true that Vlad used terror to reach his goals. He wanted to unify his country and control the wealthy boyars. It's also true that Vlad lived in a violent time. He didn't invent new forms of cruelty. The Turks executed people by impalement. So did other eastern European rulers.

But Vlad took cruelty to new heights. No one impaled people so often, or with such pleasure.

According to many accounts, Vlad liked to watch his victims die. He was a sadist, pure and simple, someone who enjoys cruelty for its own sake.

In the end, the Turks took control of Hungary in the mid-1500s. They held onto the region for more than 150 years. Wallachia, Moldavia, and Transylvania had Turkish or Russian rulers until late in the 19th century. The three states finally united and became the kingdom of Romania in 1881.

Many Romanians still see Vlad as a patriotic hero. But to most people, he will always be a symbol of terror.

Timeline of Terror

1431

1440: János Hunyadi, known as the White Knight, is selected to protect the Christian empires against the Ottoman Turks.

1444: Dracul sends his son Mircea to fight for the Holy Roman Empire at Varna.

1448: With the support of the Turks, Vlad declares himself prince of Wallachia; he stays on the throne two months.

1453: Constantinople falls to the Ottoman Turks.

1457: Vlad attacks German cities. During the Easter Massacre, Vlad slaughters the boyars of Wallachia.

1462: Vlad fights the Turks again, and the sultan retreats to Adrianople. Vlad's brother, Radu, backed by the people of Wallachia, chases Vlad out of the country.

1476: Vlad and Matthias go to war against the Turks. Later that year, Vlad takes back the Wallachian throne, but is then killed near Bucharest.

1431: Vlad Dracula is born. Vlad's father, Dracul, pledges his support to the Holy Roman Emperor and is named the prince of Wallachia.

1443–1447: Vlad and Radu are held prisoners in Adrianople, at the court of Sultan Murad.

1447: Vlad's father is killed by supporters of Vladislav II.

1452: Vlad pledges to defend the Holy Roman Empire against the Turks.

1456: Hunyadi, whom Vlad supports, saves Belgrade from the Turks. Vlad retakes the throne of Wallachia, and makes allies with rulers of the Holy Roman Empire.

1461: Vlad launches a vicious attack against the Turks, starting at Giurgiu.

1463: Vlad becomes the prisoner of King Matthias of Hungary.

1476

GLOSSARY

alliance (uh-LYE-uhnss) *noun* a friendly agreement to work together

armasi (ar-MAHS-ee) *noun* the group of soldiers who served as Vlad's executioners

assassinate (uh-SASS-uh-nate) *verb* to murder someone who is well-known or important

Black Death (BLAK DETH) *noun* another name for the bubonic plague, a disease that killed millions of people during the Middle Ages

boyars (BOI-urz) *noun* wealthy landowners in Wallachia during Vlad's time

Byzantine Empire (BIZ-uhn-teen EM-pire) *noun* the Eastern Orthodox Christian empire of the Middle Ages, centered around Constantinople

cavalry (KAV-uhl-ree) *noun* soldiers who ride on horseback

chaos (KAY-oss) *noun* total confusion

clan (KLAN) *noun* a large group of families

corpse (KORPS) *noun* a dead body, especially of a human

crusade (kroo-SADE) *noun* one of the battles fought in the Middle Ages by European Christians trying to capture lands from the Muslims

dominate (DOM-uh-nate) *verb* to control or rule

eclipse (i-KLIPS) *noun* a situation in which the moon comes between the sun and the earth so that all or part of the sun's light is blocked out

execution (ek-suh-KYOO-shun) *noun* the act of killing someone as punishment for a crime

Holy Roman Empire (HOH-lee ROH-muhn EM-pire) *noun* a Roman Catholic empire that stretched across much of central Europe during the Middle Ages

impale (im-PAIL) *verb* to torture or kill by piercing with a sharp stake

Islam (ISS-luhm) *noun* a religion based on the teachings of Muhammed

legacy (LEG-uh-see) *noun* something handed down or left behind by someone from the past

monk (MUHNGK) *noun* a man who lives in a religious community and has promised to devote his life to God

mosque (MOSK) *noun* a building used by Muslims for worship

Muslim (MUHZ-luhm) *noun* someone who follows the religion of Islam

Orthodox Christian (OR-thuh-doks KRISS-chun) *noun* a follower of the Eastern Orthodox Church, a Christian church that split from the Roman Catholic Church in 1054

Ottoman Empire (AHT-uh-mun EM-pire) *noun* a Turkish Muslim empire that began in the 1200s and gradually spread throughout much of southeastern Europe, the Middle East, and North Africa

plague (PLAYG) *noun* a very serious disease that spreads quickly to many people and often causes death

province (PROV-uhnss) *noun* a district or region of some countries

Roman Catholic (ROH-muhn KATH-uh-lik) *noun* a member of the Roman Catholic Church, a Christian church that has the pope as its leader

ruthless (ROOTH-liss) *adjective* cruel and without pity

sadistic (suh-DIST-ik) *adjective* delighting in causing pain to others

sluji (SLOO-jee) *noun* Vlad's police force

strait (STRAYT) *noun* a narrow strip of water that connects two larger bodies of water

sultan (SUHLT-uhn) *noun* an emperor or ruler of some Muslim countries

turban (TUR-buhn) *noun* a head covering made by winding a long scarf around the head

tyrant (TYE-ruhnt) *noun* someone who rules others in cruel or unjust way

viteji (VIT-uh-jee) *noun* group of officers Vlad created to lead in battle against foreign invasions

FIND OUT MORE

Here are some books and Web sites with more information about Vlad Dracula and his times.

BOOKS

Corrick, James A. **The Byzantine Empire.** Detroit: Lucent Books, 2006. (109 pages)
A clearly written account of the history of the Byzantine Empire.

Roberts, J. M. **The Illustrated History of the World, Volume IV: The Age of Diverging Traditions.** New York: Oxford University Press, 1999. (192 pages)
This richly illustrated book surveys the rise of Islam, the decline of the Byzantine Empire, and the beginning of Modern Europe.

Streissguth, Thomas. **Legends of Dracula (A & E Biography).** Minneapolis: Lerner Publications, 1999. (112 pages)
Explores how the real Dracula inspired various vampire legends, including Bram Stoker's novel.

Willis, Terri. **Romania (Enchantment of the World, Second Series).** New York: Children's Press, 2000. (114 pages) *Describes the history, geography, and culture of Romania.*

Wilson, Lionel. **The Mystery of Dracula?: Fact or Fantasy?** Morristown, NJ: Silver Burdett, 1979. (48 pages) *Discusses Bram Stoker's book as well as the historical Dracula.*

WEB SITES

http://www.bartleby.com/65/ho/HolyRoma.html
An online article about the Holy Roman Empire from the Columbia Encyclopedia.

http://www.metmuseum.org/explore/Byzantium/byz_1.html
This Metropolitan Museum of Art site is called The Glory of Byzantium.

http://www.pbs.org/frontlineworld/stories/romania/dracula1.html
This is an online companion to "Romania—My Old House," an episode of the PBS series Frontline World. *It includes facts about Vlad and an interview with a Dracula expert.*

http://www.ucs.mun.ca/~emiller/
"Dracula's Homepage," a site created by Dracula scholar Elizabeth Miller, is filled with information about the historical and fictional Draculas.

For Grolier subscribers:
http://go.grolier.com/ **searches:** Vlad the Impaler; Dracula; Romania; Ottoman Empire; Holy Roman Empire; Byzantine Empire

INDEX

Authors' Note and Bibliography

Writing about a character such as Vlad, who lived more than 500 years ago, presents a problem for the writer. How much of what is written about him is fact, and how much is fiction? We want to present a full and believable picture of the person, but we don't want to create a picture of the person if it is not accurate.

In Vlad's case, there are documents from that time, describing his life, his person, his deeds. There are letters, and there are drawings. But how do we know if these are exaggerations? Some of the stories might turn out to be just that—stories. We can't know for sure.

Nonetheless, a picture emerges. All the sources about Vlad agree that he was a powerful, ruthless, and cruel man. We can believe that there was such a man, and that he did many of the things of which he was accused.

The following books have been most useful in writing and editing Vlad's story:

Historical Biographies about Vlad Dracula

Florescu, Radu, and Raymond T. McNally. **Dracula, A Biography of Vlad the Impaler, 1431–1476.** New York: Hawthorn Books, 1973.

Florescu, Radu, and Raymond T. McNally. **Dracula: Prince of Many Faces: His Life and Times.** Boston: Little, Brown, 1989.

McNally, Raymond T., and Radu Florescu. **In Search of Dracula: The History of Dracula and Vampires.** Boston: Houghton Mifflin, 1994.

Myles, Douglas. **Prince Dracula, Son of the Devil.** New York: McGraw-Hill, 1988.

Treptow, Kurt W. **Vlad III Dracula: The Life and Times of the Historical Dracula.** Portland, OR: The Center for Romanian Studies, 2000.

Trow, M. J. **Vlad the Impaler: In Search of the Real Dracula.** Gloucestershire, UK: Sutton, 2003.

Background

The Columbia Encyclopedia, fifth edition. New York: Columbia University Press, 1993.

Novels About Dracula

Kostova, Elizabeth. **The Historian.** New York and Boston: Little Brown, 2005.

Stoker, Bram. **Dracula.** New York: New American Library, 1965. (Originally published in England, 1897.)

We are grateful to Jackie Carter, Shari Joffe, and Elizabeth Ward for their work on this project. Special thanks to our editor, Tod Olson.

—Enid A. Goldberg and Norman Itzkowitz